Library of
Davidson College

THE ROLE OF MONETARY GOLD OVER THE NEXT TEN YEARS

THE PER JACOBSSON FOUNDATION
Lecture and Commentaries

by

ALEXANDRE LAMFALUSSY
WILFRID BAUMGARTNER
GUIDO CARLI
L. K. JHA

3 p.m., Sunday, 28 September, 1969
The Great Hall — International Monetary Fund
Washington, D. C.

FOREWORD

Professor Alexandre Lamfalussy prepared, at the request of The Per Jacobsson Foundation, a substantial study on "The Role of Monetary Gold Over the Next Ten Years", to provide the basis for a discussion of the subject at the Foundation's sixth meeting, held in Washington on Sunday, 28 September, 1969. Following Professor Lamfalussy's introduction of the paper, which was distributed in advance, comments were presented by Mr. Wilfrid Baumgartner, former Minister of Finance and former Governor of the Banque de France, Governor Guido Carli of the Banca d'Italia, and Governor L. K. Jha of the Reserve Bank of India. Professor Lamfalussy responded to these comments and to written questions sent in by members of the audience. This current volume of the Proceedings contains the text of the basic study and of the discussion which followed.

This discussion is the most recent in a series organized by the Foundation in Europe, Latin America, and the United States. The papers given have been published in English, French and Spanish by the Foundation and in other languages by a number of banks, bankers' associations and others. A list of the Proceedings so far issued will be found on page 59.

The Foundation was established in 1964 in honor of Per Jacobsson, late Managing Director of the International Monetary Fund, to encourage the scholarly exploration of the international financial and monetary questions with which he was so intimately associated. Its support has come from the Fund, the World Bank, the Bank for International Settlements, and large numbers of international, governmental, corporate and private contributors led by the distinguished group of sponsors shown elsewhere in this booklet.

Table of Contents

	Page
Opening Remarks	
Pierre-Paul Schweitzer, Managing Director, International Monetary Fund	1
W. Randolph Burgess, President, The Per Jacobsson Foundation	1
The Role of Monetary Gold Over The Next Ten Years	
Alexandre Lamfalussy	
Introduction and Summary	3
Text	10
Commentaries	
Wilfrid Baumgartner	33
Guido Carli	35
L. K. Jha	43
Questions and Answers	
Professor Lamfalussy	47
Governor Jha	50
Mr. Schweitzer	51
Mr. Burgess	52
Appendices	
1. Biographies of Speakers	53
2. List of Sponsors, Directors and Officers of the Foundation	55
3. List of Publications	59

OPENING REMARKS

Pierre-Paul Schweitzer:

Ladies and gentlemen, it is really a great privilege to welcome you here on behalf of the International Monetary Fund and The Per Jacobsson Foundation. You know what Per Jacobsson represented for me, as an example and inspiration; and you certainly share my emotions today.

We were sorry that Mrs. Violet Jacobsson could not attend this time. We all know that she is with us in heart this afternoon, and I am happy that so many other members of the family are here. It is a great pleasure to welcome them here today.

There have already been several lectures, but this is the first time that they have taken place in the building of the International Monetary Fund, which is a very suitable place to hold them. We are happy to be able to welcome you here.

I won't take any more time from the speakers, and I now hand over the proceedings to Ambassador Burgess.

W. Randolph Burgess:

Let me start by welcoming you all here on behalf of The Per Jacobsson Foundation, and particularly by thanking Pierre-Paul Schweitzer and the Monetary Fund for the great courtesies extended to us, not only in making available this beautiful hall, but more so in their constant support of the Foundation. We could not get along without the constant support of the International Monetary Fund and we want to thank them most cordially for it, not only on behalf of the Foundation but on behalf of the members of the Jacobsson family who have always been so cordially welcomed in the Fund.

I am sorry to say Mrs. Per Jacobsson is not able to be here, but many of the other representatives of the family are, and we particularly welcome them here.

You have had in your hands the very interesting paper prepared by Professor Lamfalussy and I know you have all studied it carefully. This paper was written a number of weeks ago; since that time a number of things have happened to the monetary system of the world, and I think Professor Lamfalussy may want to say something about those events and may want to add some punctuation here and there.

Professor Lamfalussy, we are delighted to have you. We are most grateful to you for preparing this paper, and we will listen intently to what you have to add to it.

THE ROLE OF MONETARY GOLD OVER THE NEXT TEN YEARS

by

ALEXANDRE LAMFALUSSY

In response to the invitation extended to him by the Foundation, Professor Lamfalussy prepared a written study on this subject which was distributed in advance to those attending the lecture meeting. The text of this paper begins on page 10. At the meeting, Professor Lamfalussy introduced his paper in the statement below.

I would like first to sum up very shortly the thesis which I developed in my paper and then to restate it; because, despite some recent developments, I have not changed my views; yet I think it might be worthwhile to reformulate the various points I developed in a slightly different way and then perhaps to spell out a certain number of policy conclusions by being more explicit than I was in my paper.

I started off by observing recent trends in monetary history and I have come to the conclusion that we have been moving towards a gradual demonetization of gold. Why this conclusion? We can observe that gold has not contributed to the growth of international liquidity any longer since about ten years. We have watched the establishment and the functioning of the dual gold market. We have seen, moreover, that the gold price on the "free market" did not rise to a level which had been expected by many people and that, after having reached a maximum of about 45 dollars, it has in fact tended to decline over the last few months. Finally, we are now approaching the creation of SDRs which is also, in a certain way, a further step towards the demonetization of gold.

The question which I then raised in my paper was whether this was likely to continue, for I think that the facts which I have just mentioned can hardly be questioned. My answer was very explicitly no: we will not make further progress on the road towards demonetization until we succeed in improving, and very substantially improving, the adjustment mechanism and, at the same time, in creating in an orderly way an adequate amount of new international liquidity.

Now on both these points, but especially on the first one—on the adjustment mechanism—, I was and still am rather pessimistic. I do not think that the adjustment mechanism, as it has been working over the last five or ten years, has improved. On the contrary, I think it is becoming less and less effective. I quoted a certain number of facts to that effect in my paper. The reasons I saw were basically of three kinds:
—One, the necessity to maintain the domestic responsibilities of governments in a changing institutional framework.
—Second, the doubts about the gradual adjustment in the current account through relative changes in unit costs.
—And third, the growing importance of capital flows and their interconnection with flows in trade and services.

As regards the second condition, I have pointed out a certain number of signs of a shortage of international liquidity. I know this is not a very fashionable view, but I tried to support it by quoting two series of facts: First, the spreading of controls all over the world, especially controls on capital flows, which certainly can be regarded as a sign of shortage of international liquidity. Second, the war of escalation in interest rates. I do not doubt that the increases in interest rates have been motivated to some extent and in some cases by purely domestic considerations—the fight against the overheating of the economy—but I simply cannot believe that the rise in interest rates would have been of the size and of the speed which actually occurred had it not been for balance-of-payments considerations or, more exactly, because of the governments wanting to preserve their foreign exchange reserves. This, I think, is a clear indication of an insufficiency of international liquidity.

The upshot of all this is that unless we get a fundamental improvement on both these counts, we will not move towards a gradual and orderly demonetization of gold but much more likely towards more controls, or towards the dollar standard, or probably towards both at the same time. I suggested some good or bad reasons which made me dislike both of these alternatives and especially their simultaneous occurrence. This led me, quite logically I believe, to the suggestion that the only way out is to improve the flexibility of exchange rates.

May I perhaps now restate this thesis in a slightly different way? When I re-read my own paper after three months, I asked myself the question which probably many of you are tempted to ask: if our present monetary system is so deficient, how could it function so well for the last twenty-five years? For there is little doubt that the system has been quite successful. Economic growth has rarely been so strong, so sustained, and so regular as over the last twenty-five years. We have had a tremendous expansion in international trade, and this continues. And we *do* have—even after the reimposition of certain controls—a fair degree of freedom in international capital transactions. So, by all three of these criteria, the system proved to be successful.

Nevertheless, I am ready to argue that some very fundamental changes have taken place in the world economy which create entirely new conditions. Hence, the fact that our present system has worked well until recently does not imply that it will work well in the future.

Which are these changes? I try to sum them up without attaching any importance to the order in which I will mention them.

The first of these changes is the very substantial increase in domestic liquidity, first of all in the sheer actual volume of domestic liquid assets. You can take any of the developed countries over the last ten or fifteen years and you can see that the total amount of domestic liquidity as expressed in national currency has been multiplied by two, three, four, five, depending on the definition that you use. This is due partly to the stock of money and partly to the stock of quasi-money and of other semi-liquid financial assets. But, in addition to the sheer quantitative expansion of liquidity, you must take into account the qualitative changes within domestic financial organizations: the increased intermediation which creates greater flexibility and hence a greater degree of liquidity within the economy. I think this is something absolutely fundamental if you compare today's position with what existed twenty or twenty-five years ago.

A second equally important point is the liberalization of capital movements. When the present system was created, the liberalization of capital movements was considered as a very, very distant objective, the main objective being the liberalization of trade. Since 1958, we have acquired a fair degree of freedom in capital transactions. This freedom has now been curtailed to some extent but it still exists and it does exist in some new form through the Euro-currency market.

The third point which is worth mentioning is the speed and the spread of financial information. With the development of a new type of journalism, with the speed of information in general, we have reached a sort of financial integration through radio, telex and television which was absolutely unheard of a few years ago. I remember watching television over the last few months, and the kind of financial information they give bears no comparison with what existed twenty years ago.

The fourth major change which I would like to point out is the growing interpenetration of the Western economies. This applies quite obviously, of course, and I hardly need to mention it, to trade flows, but it also applies to direct investment through the substantial development of the multi-national corporations and, last but not least, to tourist trade. Millions of people traveling from one country to another, knowing the price structure of each of the countries, comparing the national standards of living—all of these factors really have created a degree of interpenetration of the Western world which was totally nonexistent twenty years ago.

Now consider all these facts at the same time: growth of domestic liquidity, hence the growth of the funds which can be shifted quickly from one country to another in case of capital movements; second, the freedom to do so directly or indirectly through the Euro-dollar market; third, the degree of information on whether this happens and through which channels; and fourth, the degree of interpenetration of our economies. You come obviously to the conclusion that we have much greater potential and real capital movements than a number of years ago. Hence I think that the old philosophy of balance-of-payments adjustment alone or principally through trade adjustment is really something which is entirely out of date and has nothing to do with current economic conditions. I also think that an institutional framework which is built primarily on a sort of "current account philosophy" is also out of date.

This is one set of facts which explain why the problem did not exist ten, fifteen or twenty years ago and why it has grown gradually into the situation which we experience today.

There are, however, a second series of facts which we have to take into account: we have been moving away from the synchronization of economic trends in a number of countries, especially within Continental Europe. When you look today at the European economies, you find that national trends become stronger and stronger and the sort of harmonization of economic development which we did have between 1959 and 1963-64 has absolutely vanished. We have special problems in France, we have special problems in Italy, we have special problems in Germany, in Belgium. You cannot point out one single country which is moving really in unison with the others.

Should one regard this as a consequence of the lack of coordination of economic policies? To this very important question, my answer would be rather dubitative. It may be that we did not manage our economies well enough or that we did not succeed in coordinating economic policies in an efficient way; but my suspicion is rather that we are in the presence of strong political and social trends in each of our countries, which go against the growing internationalization of the economy. I suggest that a large part of our problems have been brought about by this divorce between the fundamental interpenetration of our economies and the persistence and strengthening of social and political trends in individual countries. I do not know whether these trends are something fundamental, or whether they are purely accidental or whether they are due to sheer bad luck. Whatever their nature or causes, one cannot doubt their existence. This is why I believe so strongly that, in order to reconcile these two fundamental trends, both of which are facts of life, we have to find some sort of compromise, and I cannot see any other compromise than a greater flexibility in exchange rates.

But what kind of flexibility? I do not intend to answer this question fully because I do not know the answer. Nevertheless, I might perhaps spell out very shortly my own prejudices or policy preferences. In theory, I would have a preference for the IMF kind of flexibility; in other words, for fixed exchange rates with periodic adjustments in case of basic imbalance. If the countries which in fact incur basic imbalances

decided to devalue or revalue when it was needed, I think the IMF system could function perfectly well. It did function in some instances, especially in the cases of smaller countries, but we have had at least two or three major cases over the last few years when devaluations did not take place or took place only too late, and we have at least one major case where a re-evaluation, at least until today, has not taken place. Hence the conclusion that, despite all the advantages of the IMF system, we may have to find something else, because the experience seems to suggest that the countries are unable or unwilling to make the system work. This is why we may have to fall back on some sort of second-best, perhaps on a widening of the band plus some sort of dynamic and crawling changes in the band itself. I think this is probably the direction we ought to take. This sounds fairly pessimistic, because the technical feasibility of such a system is still questionable, and yet I think that, by necessity, we will be driven to a solution of this kind.

However, I would not like to end my talk simply by being so acutely pessimistic. I think we have two reasons for being somewhat optimistic. The one is that all these problems are those of a growing society, of a growing economy. These are not problems of a declining world. We tend to forget it sometimes, but this is a very important fact. Our problems are the result of conflicting trends: national independence and growing internationalization. Both these conflicts and their solution are part of the process of growth.

My second reason for hope is that we are beginning to understand the mechanics of international payments and that our own minds are also changing. The proof for this is that the SDRs are on the verge of being accepted and that the idea of a greater flexibility of exchange rates meets an increasingly positive reception.

May I conclude by reading you a few sentences which I found in a preface written by John Maynard Keynes to his *Monetary Reform* in October 1923? I quote: "Nowhere do conservative notions consider themselves more in place than in currency, yet nowhere is the need of innovation more urgent. One is often warned that a scientific treatment of currency questions is impossible because the banking world is intellectually incapable of understanding its own problems. If this is true, the order of society which they stand for will decay. But I do not believe it. If the new ideas now developing in many quarters are sound and right, I do not doubt that sooner or later they will prevail. Hence I dedicate this book humbly and without permission to the Governors of the Bank of England who now and for the future have a much more difficult task entrusted to them than in former days."

I would like to paraphrase this and say that I dedicate this talk very humbly and entirely without permission to the Governors of the International Monetary Fund.

THE ROLE OF MONETARY GOLD OVER THE NEXT TEN YEARS

by

ALEXANDRE LAMFALUSSY

The text below is that of the written paper prepared by Professor Lamfalussy and circulated in advance to those attending the meeting. The text of his oral presentation of this paper begins on page 3.

The task which has been assigned to me is of undoubtedly complex nature. To discuss the long-term prospects of the monetary function of gold implies not only economic analysis but also political considerations, and even speculation about human nature. Essentially, monetary management is an act of policy as well as political action; international monetary management is even more so. The attitude towards gold is often determined, among political men, central bankers, private bankers or just ordinary private people, by motivations which the economist is unable to assess and which belong more to the field of a sociologist or a psychologist. However, this paper is that of an economist, influenced by his experience as a banker, and we all know how the expert can simplify when he has to deal with something outside his own field.

Then, there is the problem of forecasting. We have only to consider the succession of crises during the last four years, each of which cast a doubt, in a more or less unexpected manner, on various points of the international monetary system as well as on the currency of different countries, to realize the extreme fragility of any attempt to forecast. Furthermore, I have but few illusions on my own capacity as a forecaster: strictly speaking, therefore, I will not make any actual forecasts but rather a series of comments on the present situation and on how it *might* evolve. For the purpose of provoking and sustaining discussion, I intend to be explicit and argumentative.

Finally, with a subject like this, which touches all aspects of social and political life, it is very difficult to draw a demarcation line between analysis and value judgements, between forecasts and wishful thinking. You have therefore the right to know my own policy preferences. They are of two kinds. On the one hand, I would like to see gold lose its monetary function; on the other, however, I would *not* like a national currency to assume the rôle of a reserve and international currency, that is to say, that the unsteady gold-exchange standard be replaced by the dollar standard. Consequently, I would like that the demonetization of gold takes place alongside with the creation of an international reserve currency. At the risk of repeating myself, I would emphasize that these are my wishes and not my forecasts.

The present situation: an interpretation

We commence our analysis by a brief examination of the gold and foreign exchange assets held by the official institutions. Throughout this report, I will refer to these reserves as the international liquidity, except where expressly re-defined. This definition of international liquidity is somewhat restrictive; it is not what I would like to use, in principle. The ideal definition would cover a much wider notion: in the case of an individual country, its total means of payment, acceptable for international settlements, which the monetary authorities of that country could raise at very short notice. This amount should include not only owned reserves but also borrowing capacity, fast and unconditional, with other official institutions or international bodies. In the extreme, it should even include the capacity to borrow on the Euro-currency and Euro-bond markets. Unfortunately, it is impossible to assess a figure for such a wide definition of international liquidity with sufficient accuracy: thus we propose that we should simply use the definition of *International Financial Statistics* which, though restrictive, is at least clear-cut. The IMF definition has the additional merit of limiting the concept of international liquidity to the amount of reserves over which the monetary authorities of a country have unconditional and immediate command. This is not without importance in a era dominated by vast and swift movements of capital, when speculative attitudes are strongly influenced by the confidence (or lack of confidence) one can have in the ability of the national authorities to settle their debts immediately and unconditionally (*).

Table I.

Amount and composition of reserves held by official institutions

(World total, at the end of the year, in billions of U.S. dollars)

	1958	1963	1968
Gold	38.0	40.2	38.9
Foreign currencies	17.0	22.2	30.9
Reserve positions with the International Monetary Fund	2.6	3.9	6.5
Total	57.6	66.4	76.3

Source: International Financial Statistics

The striking fact apparent from this Table is that over the last ten years, gold has practically no longer contributed to the growth of international liquidity. In ten years, total foreign reserves rose by nearly 19 billion dollars; the greater part of this increase—some 14 billion—was due to increased holdings in foreign currencies, whereas the increase in the reserve positions with the International Monetary Fund was about 4 billion. The increase in gold stocks was less than one billion; in fact, there was a decline between 1963 and 1968. Consequently, the share of gold holdings in total reserves, which was 66 per cent at the end of 1958, fell to 51 per cent at the end of 1968.

Two other facts should also be taken into account, though they are not apparent from the Table. First, there was a considerable slowing down in the growth of international liquidity between 1965 and the middle of 1968. At the end of 1965, the amount of reserves was 70.4 billion dollars; it reached barely 73 billion by the end of June 1968.

(*) On this point, as on some other, I published a recent article in the December 1968 number of the *"Recherches Économiques de Louvain"*.

Between these two dates the yearly growth rate was therefore less than 2 per cent. During the last six months of 1968, there was a considerable rise in foreign currency holdings but, to a large extent, this was a "negotiated" increase and not the result of the traditional functioning of the gold-exchange standard.

It is precisely this second fact which must be emphasized, as it cannot be seen from the Fund's statistics. During the last five years, the amount of foreign currencies held by official institutions went up by some 9 billion dollars: but this increase is not the result of the mechanics of the gold-exchange standard. This system creates reserves under the impact of the overall deficit of the balance of payments of the United States (or the United Kingdom) whose currencies are held spontaneously by the surplus countries. However, as was shown by Professor Triffin in a recent statistical note (March, 1969), the whole of the 9 billion increase—in fact more than this increase—must be attributed to *negotiated* currency holdings. In adopting this method of calculation, we arrive at the conclusion that, at the end of 1968, foreign currency holdings of the "spontaneous" gold-exchange standard type now represent only about 13 to 14 billion dollars, that is approximately the same amount as at the end of 1958. The negotiated holdings in foreign currencies amounted at the same date to 16 or 17 billion dollars. By adding this amount to that of the reserve positions with the International Monetary Fund, we could say therefore (a) that between 1958 and 1968, the *whole* of the increase of the international liquidity must be attributed to the *negotiated* creation of reserves either in foreign currencies or in the reserve positions with the Monetary Fund, since neither gold nor foreign currency held spontaneously have contributed to the growth of reserves and (b) that at the end of the period, the negotiated reserves represented about 30 per cent of total international liquidity.

It is therefore right to say that over the last ten years and in particular since 1963-64, we have witnessed a gradual decline in the role of gold as a means of reserve and its complete disappearance as a source of *new* international liquidity. At the same time, the mechanics of the gold-exchange standard have ceased to function: the creation of reserves by the spontaneous holding of dollars or Sterling has come to a halt and has been replaced by the creation of negotiated reserves. Finally, if we disregard the rapid growth of reserves in the last half of 1968, there has been a clear slowing down in the expansion of international liquidity since 1965.

This diagnosis of the present situation, based on facts and figures, should be supplemented by considerations of another kind, no less important but of more controversial nature. They touch upon the operation of the gold market and on the attitude towards the United States dollar.

The present organization of the gold market, the two-tier system, owes its origin to the waves of speculation against the dollar and in favour of a re-valuation of gold, which culminated in the March 1968 crisis. Its principal characteristic is the isolation of the ordinary gold market from that of monetary gold. The monetary price of gold remains fixed at 35 dollars per ounce and it is at this price that the central banks trade between themselves, and mainly with the Federal Reserve. The price on the ordinary market is fixed freely by supply and demand. The two markets are cut off from each other as the majority of the large central banks have agreed to refrain from purchasing or selling gold on the ordinary market.

We all know the discussions which have surrounded these measures, the ambiguity of the commitments of some of the central banks, the talks between the United States and South Africa on the latter's sales of gold, the uncertainty regarding the survival of the system. It is not our intention to enter the debate at this stage. Let us, however, put forward a fundamental proposition. *The establishment of a two-tier system is an important step towards the demonetization of gold.* This proposition is not meant to speculate about the intentions of those who, by their decisions, have set up the new system; it simply brings to your notice its implications, assuming, of course, that the system survives. The first implication is that the gold part of the reserves cannot be increased, for lack of purchasing from the ordinary market. As nobody doubts the need for increasing international liquidity, this entails inevitably the relative narrowing of the gold basis. In other words, the trends observed in fact between 1958 and 1968 would continue in the future. Second conclusion: the prices on the two markets may only be the same by pure accident. This not to say that the price on the "ordinary" market is the "real price" (*) but the absence of purchases and sales outside the circuit of the central banks implies in return that the price of monetary gold has become purely arbitrary. Thus, in the logic of the system, gold becomes a unit of account, destined to fulfill less and less the function of a means of reserve and practically not at all that of a means of settlement of debts between central banks. For this reason, it would seem legitimate to us to say that the system of a double gold market, by extrapolating the trends already noticed for ten years, confirms and foreshadows the decline—the "withering away" —of the monetary function of gold.

The more recent events on the gold market seem to confirm this diagnosis, although one can be never too careful in interpreting the short-term fluctuation of a market which has proved to be remarkably volatile in the past. During the months of April, May and June of this year, the price of ordinary gold tended to decline and fell to nearly 41 dollars these last few days (**). This fall would not be worth mentioning if it were not for the fact that it coincided with the announcement of a sizable deterioration in the United States balance of payments and especially in the most significant part of this, that is in the current account. Whereas twelve months previously much more favourable balance-of-payments figures hardly prevented heavy speculation against the dollar, data which are much worse are now accompanied by a fall in the price of ordinary gold! Does this mean that the two-tier system is finally accepted? Is this due to a rather hasty interpretation of the impact of South African gold sales on the Swiss market? Or is this fall to be attributed simply to the very high interest rates on short-term dollar deposits? We will revert to this curious development later. In the meantime, we will simply note the fact and consider it as a preliminary indication that the decline of the monetary function of gold is on its way and that it is accompanied by a considerable strengthening of the position of the dollar.

This interpretation of past events and of the present situation is, of course, not to everybody's taste. Although not denying the facts and

(*) Even in the absence of effective purchases or sales on this market by the central banks, this price would only become the "true" price if all the buyers and sellers of the metal acquired the conviction that no central bank will ever connect the two markets in any way. As long as this conviction does not exist—and it does not appear to exist to-day—the price on the ordinary market will take into account potential purchases and sales by the official institutions. Quite clearly, the market is at the moment discounting possible purchases (rather than sales) by the central banks.

(**) The first half of June, 1969.

figures mentioned above nor the rapid degeneration of the gold-exchange standard, some economists—and particularly French ones—insist on the repeated monetary crises of the last four years and on the generalization of foreign exchange controls. Because of these, they give quite a different interpretation to the facts mentioned in the preceding pages. According to them, the stagnation of official gold holdings, until measures were taken in March 1968, was caused precisely by the public's mistrust of the system: it is the private hoarding of gold which was preventing the central banks from making gold pay its role as creator of international reserves. It is this same mistrust which made it impossible for the gold-exchange standard to function properly and which therefore led to the "negotiated" creation of reserves. Seen from this point of view, the establishment of the two-tier system is an act of despair, the survival of which is more than doubtful. Instead of a decline of the monetary function of gold, we are on the road to more frequent monetary crises, to exchange restrictions of all kinds and finally to a collapse of the economy—which could be avoided only by the re-establishment of the gold standard.

It is obvious to me that both interpretations have some merit. They are not in basic opposition over the explanation of past and even present facts: for example, it would be difficult to deny that the stagnation of the gold holdings of the central banks, between 1963 and March 1968, was due to the increase in gold hoarding. Furthermore, it cannot be denied that the setting up of a two-tier system in the Spring of 1968 was an act of defense by the central banks which had no desire to lose even more gold. Having said this, however, it must be admitted, on the other hand, that *de facto* the monetary role of gold has diminished. The divergence, therefore, lies not so much in the interpretation of what has happened so far, as in *forecasting* the future.

I have no intention of entering the game of forecasting in the proper sense of the term, for I have no idea what will *actually* happen to the monetary function of gold in the future, and I do not even see ways and means of working out sensible forecasts in this field. Hence the rest of the paper will deal with the future in a more policy-oriented way. I will try to answer the following question: what conditions are required for past trends to be continued? In other words: under what conditions can we expect the decline in the monetary function of gold to continue and to end in the effective de-monetization of gold?

*Two conditions: improvement of the adjustment process
and creation of international liquidity*

These requirements are of two kinds: the adequate functioning of the adjustment process and the creation of sufficient international liquidity. These two problems, of course, are interdependent: the need for external reserves is a function, partially at least, of the speed of the adjustment process, while this latter also depends, to some extent, on the amount of reserves available which can hasten or slow down the use of appropriate adjustment policies. For the purposes of this report, however, I will deal with these two problems one after the other, beginning with the adjustment process.

Whatever the outcome, we may assume that if these two conditions are not satisfied, the decline in the monetary function of gold cannot continue. Both lasting disequilibria in external balances (i.e. the weakness or inexistence of the adjustment process) and the shortage of international liquidity are apt to create an economic climate dominated by uncertainty, speculation, controls and crises, which are hardly likely to encourage the decline of the monetary function of gold. Such events are likely to push up the price of gold on the free market and this, in the long run and in case of a persistent and substantial difference between the market price and 35 dollars, could break the clear separation between the two markets.

The problem of the adjustment process

It is not easy to sum up our experience of the adjustment process over the last, say, fifteen years. There are, on the one hand, a number of *small* countries which have had a fairly satisfactory experience: these include Holland, Belgium, Switzerland and some Scandinavian countries which have had substantial changes in their balances of payments without the persistence of prolonged surplus or deficit positions. In this category we could include, among the large countries, Japan (with large and rapid variations of its external balances) and, to a lesser extent, Italy (which, however, had only one period of heavy deficit, in 1963-64). On the other hand, we have three *large* countries—the United States, the United Kingdom and Western Germany—where the adjustment process seems to have failed to function entirely (United States) or worked only in a very unsatisfactory manner (United Kingdom and Western Germany). This classification involves an implicit definition of the satisfactory functioning of the adjustment process: the absence of large and durable deficits or surpluses.

Events of the last eighteen months have revived anxiety over the proper functioning of the adjustment process. The huge surplus in the balance of current transactions of Western Germany has been maintained in spite of the considerable expansion of domestic expenditure; the deficit in the British balance of payments has not been reduced at the rate expected in spite of a strongly deflationary fiscal policy; neither has the American economy responded to the fiscal measures introduced there more than a year ago, nor up to this date (mid June, 1969) to a policy of monetary restriction. In the case of France, the exchange control has, in fact, replaced the use of adjustment policies.

The delays in the adjustment process may be localized in five phases or points of impact:

(1) Delays in the use of the appropriate restrictive or expansionary policies.

(2) The application of an appropriate monetary *or* fiscal policy, the effects of which are, however, cancelled or weakened by a compensating policy in another field (e.g. the effects of a restrictive fiscal policy offset by an expansionary monetary policy, or vice versa.

(3) The domestic expenditure—consumption or investment, or both —fail to adjust to the measures taken.

(4) In the *balance on current account,* compensation between the price and income effects; I have in mind here, for instance, a country whose economy is in strong recovery, yet where the growth of home demand, in full expansion, does not reduce the surplus on current account as it is accompanied by a net improvement in the country's competitive position which stems from an accelerated growth of productivity.

(5) Capital movements aggravating or prolonging the deficit, increasing the surplus or making it last longer, or offsetting any tendency of the current account to return to equilibrium.

Of these various causes of delay in the adjustment process, numbers (2) and (3) will perhaps give less trouble in the future than in the past. Perhaps I am rather optimistic in this regard, but it would not seem to me to be rash to state that some definite progress has been made recently in the proper use of the "policy mix." Having overcome the apparent contradiction between oversimplified Keynesian and quantity theories of money, the majority of economists and experts now recognize as valid either the *simultaneous* use of monetary and fiscal policies or, at least, the necessity to avoid any "perverse" compensation. We admit that we know little of consumers' reactions as we do not know whether they more willingly accept to change their propensity to save or the velocity of circulation of money. In case of doubt, we prefer therefore to place them in a situation where an absence of reaction on their part to fiscal and monetary stimulants would bring about a simultaneous change of the *two* coefficients—hardly a plausible assumption and rarely encountered in economic history. We have the impression therefore that governments will, in the future, pay more attention to ensure that the two policies are applied simultaneously, or at least in a co-ordinated way. In this case, it could also be expected that home demand will react with greater speed to rational and concerted policy injunctions.

Unfortunately, this relative optimism can hardly be extended to the other three causes of the improper functioning of the adjustment mechanism. The delay in the application of the appropriate policies or simply the refusal to allow the external surplus or deficit to act on home demand originates in the majority of cases from the traditional conflict of objectives of economic policy between domestic and external equilibrium. It would appear from the policies of most governments that their concern with domestic equilibrium still has priority over the balance of payments and that they are not ready—or not able—to abandon this attitude. It is characteristic to note that the present Administration of the United States, while recognizing the necessity to combat inflation, is in no position to acknowledge (publicly) the need for increasing unemployment, and that businessmen—who expect a swift and vigorous expansionist intervention of the Federal Authorities in the event of a recession—already look *beyond* such "temporary" recession. In the circumstances, it is not surprising that investment expenditure shows no signs of decline. It is also interesting to note that the revaluation of the Deutsche Mark—a tool of adjustment policy *par excellence*—has become an electoral question; and we are told of the "sacrifices" Germans must take in the event of a revaluation of their currency, whereas a first year student could show you that a revaluation implies (assuming no change in the rate of use of resources) an *increase* in real income for the country which revalues. Indeed, it could not be otherwise: since how could there be sacrifices (this time real ones) in the event of a *de*valuation if somebody did not benefit from an advantage? There are many such assertions that could be quoted almost daily proving that the concern with domestic equilibrium (whether well- or ill-conceived) is growing rather than declining. This is the main reason for my belief that we should not expect more rapid application of the appropriate adjustment policies, especially when they risk causing domestic difficulties which would be politically harmful to the government in power.

Scepticism should also be expressed as regards any future improvement in the adjustment process achieved indirectly from the *relative changes* in the unit cost of labour, that is to say by suppressing perverse developments of the type mentioned under heading (4) above. It is often said that a rise in wages as well as that of productivity are universal phenomena: consequently, a country suffering from a competitive disadvantage could improve its position (without devaluing) by slowing down the rise in its labour unit costs relative to the unit costs of its competitors. My scepticism of this gradual adjustment process is based on two considerations. First, on my belief that there are genuinely vicious or "virtuous" circles in increases of productivity, probably *via* the volume, the quality and the distribution by industry of investments. This implies that a rapid rate of growth of productivity creates conditions which lead to further rises in productivity, and vice versa: we need only consider the case of Germany and Japan, in one sense, and that of Great Britain, in the other. The second observation is derived from the almost universal failure of income and especially wages policies: experience has shown that it is the relation between supply and demand which fixes the level and rate of increase of wages. These two observations, combined, show clearly the extreme fragility of any hopes of an adjustment based on the gradual changes of relative unit costs. As an example, I would quote the case of a non-competitive country which hopes to improve its relative competitive position. If it slows down its growth, it will perhaps manage to put a brake on the rise of wages but at the cost of slowing down the rise in productivity; on the other hand if it decides to push ahead in the hope of using its productive capacities to the fullest possible extent (the French *"fuite en avant"*) and thus increases its productivity, it risks upsetting its labour market. In both cases, adjustment will be doubtful or in any case very slow.

Finally, de-stabilizing capital movements are likely to *increase* in the future rather than to diminish. First, because of the constant rise in the volume of *domestic* liquid assets in all countries. Second, owing to the acceleration of the information process and means of communication leading to an ever larger and quicker diffusion of economic news, opinions and even expectations. Third, through the increasing interconnection between the flow of funds in the balance of current transactions and those linked with capital movements.

This latter source of instability deserves a brief examination apart. It implies that governments are hardly any longer in a position of controlling capital movements for the simple reason that it has become increasingly difficult to identify capital transactions and to distinguish them from operations on current account.

A possible source of confusion between the two is the ever increasing amount of tourist traffic which few governments are ready to hamper. Travel can lead to considerable flows of capital, *via* transactions in banknotes, and these can only be stopped either by a strict control at the border or by having a special floating exchange rate for banknotes. Italy's balance of payments is an excellent example of how much capital can be exported through the sales of banknotes. Possibilities of the same nature exist in all those European countries where banknotes form a substantial proportion of the stock of money. There are many of them.

The second possibility of confusion and the more important one, between current transactions and movements of capital, arises from the increasing share of *intra*-firm settlements of the large multinational companies in *inter*national trade. These companies pay much attention to the optimum use of their cash reserves which are usually managed at top level, without decentralization. This practice is apt to lead to very large capital movements in at least three ways. First, by substantial *leads and lags*. Second, by shifting the localization of the financing of trade between subsidiaries: changes are made easily from the financing of exports to imports, or vice versa, whenever the interest rates make it slightly more advantageous to borrow in one country rather than in the other, or at the first signs of uncertainty as regards the stability of exchange rates. It is, of course, true that these are once-for-all changes. But there is a third route open to multinational companies to transfer capital through foreign trade: the flows may be changed—and this time in a lasting manner—by adapting prices at which the transactions between the subsidiaries are settled. Most of these prices are arbitrary, especially where products are exchanged which do not have a clear market price: this is the case for a large number of intermediary products. It is precisely this difficulty of defining the profit of a local operation which induces most of the multinational companies to be opposed to minority shareholdings in the stock capital of a subsidiary. Profit only has a meaning where it is meant to be maximized, that is to say for the company *as a whole*. The upshot of all this is that even in theory, the distinction between current and capital transactions becomes more and more difficult; and, in practice, both the statistician and the government agency in charge of foreign exchange controls will find it exceedingly difficult to distinguish trade from capital flows. This is the price to pay for the growing integration of the Western world.

Capital movements of this kind will, of course, not *always* go against the adjustment process. But they are likely to do so in many instances, especially when holders of liquid assets either do not believe in the government's willingness (or ability) to apply an appropriate policy of adjustment or do not expect such policy to be successful. Hence our general conclusion: in our present system, where exchange rates appear to have acquired considerable rigidity, the process of adjustment should not be expected to accelerate. On the contrary, it is likely to lengthen and become less effective.

Shortage of international liquidity?

There is no general agreement on a simple way of measuring whether there is adequate international liquidity or not. The Ossola Report in 1965 suggested a series of symptoms which, if they were to appear simultaneously, could be taken as a sign of a shortage of external reserves: the generalization of restrictions on payments and international trade, the instability of exchange rates, the decline of international prices, the increase in unemployment. At the moment of writing (June, 1969), there is certainly no sign of a generalization of the last two symptoms, although many economists are counting on their appearance. There also appears to be no effective instability of exchange rates—but there is no doubt that they are *potentially* instable. The first sympton, on the other hand, is undeniably present: France and the United Kingdom apply a rigorous exchange control; the United States have been using various means for many years to control the capital outflow; Italy has recently introduced measures the practical effect of which has been to reduce capital exports; Belgium has a system of double exchange rates and, as a result of this, capital exports have been penalized, since about nine months, by a "dollar premium" of 6 to 8 per cent; Germany has introduced fiscal measures in order to reduce the surplus of its balance of payments. All these measures indicate clearly that governments are more and more concerned with the state of their balance of payments and that the preservation of external reserves has acquired priority over other policy objectives.

The "competitive" rise in interest rates confirms the current importance of the balance of payments in economic policy. Of course, the series of increases of the discount rates in a number of European countries, since the Autumn 1968, *also* fulfil the task to moderate the domestic overheating of the economy; but these rises would not have been so frequent or substantial if there had not been the need to check the outflow of capital attracted by the very high interest rates in the United States and on the Euro-dollar market. In this sense the war of escalation in discount rates shows the shortage of reserves: it makes it obvious that the freedom of action of governments to apply an autonomous domestic policy has become very limited, indeed more limited than most of the democratically elected governments would be ready (or could afford) to accept.

As regards the quantitative basis of measuring the reserve needs, there is no agreement either between the experts. At the most, it is admitted that in the long run there must be a positive relation between the growth of reserves and that of international trade.

I think, however, that we could go further by suggesting that *the level* of external reserves should remain in a more or less constant relation

with the total of the *domestic* liquid assets. This proposal is derived from the following reasoning:
(1) The main function of external reserves is to assure governments a certain freedom of action in national economic policy. This is accomplished by the financing of deficits in the balance of payments which are temporary, unexpected or tolerated for other policy reasons, while awaiting for the adjustment process to re-establish the external equilibrium. The need for reserves is therefore a function of the frequency, size and duration of external deficits.
(2) We have seen that two dominant facts seem to characterize the world today:
   (a) the inevitable and often unexpected nature of capital movements involving exceedingly large amounts and the difficulty of separating them from current transactions;
   (b) the lengthening of the adjustment process either because of these same capital flows or for political and social reasons, making a return to balance in the current account itself both slow and arduous.
(3) The deficits the financing of which has to be provided for by means of drawings on the reserves are therefore those of the balance of payments as a whole, including both current and capital accounts.
(4) It is reasonable to assume that where there is freedom in international transactions, the probability of balance-of-payments deficits increases with the growth of domestic liquid assets. It may also be expected that the duration of these deficits, that is to say the slowing down of the adjustment process, will also depend on the amount of national liquidities and (perhaps even more) on the degree of liquidity of the economy. This probability does not concern only capital movements defined conventionally but also real or fictitious current transactions. The extent of the leads and lags in trade payments—as also the accumulation of stocks of imported products—is clearly a function of the volume of liquid assets held by firms and households. The same stands for the possibility for them to export capital in the traditional sense of the term.

A comparison of the amount of external reserves with that of national liquid assets shows, over time, a considerable change in the relation between these two important items. Table II/a, which shows the volume of external reserves as a percentage of the *stock of money*, informs us of the decline in these ratios for all the countries listed, the only exception being France which, however, had notoriously insufficient reserves at the end of 1958.

It may be seen from this table that the lowest ratios, at the end of 1968, were those for the United States, the United Kingdom, France and Japan. No wonder that three out of these four countries maintain strict foreign exchange controls and that the fourth (the United States) uses all available means short of an exchange control in the technical sense to prevent capital exports. In these four countries, it would only be necessary for the stock of money (defined in its narrow sense) to drop by some 7 to 8 per cent following a deficit in the balance of payments, for the financing of it to absorb all external reserves. It may be argued, of course, that such a fall in the stock of money could hardly happen without setting into motion the adjustment process, by raising interest rates or directly affecting national expenditure. However, two

Table II/a.

	External reserve ratios	
	1958	1968
United States	15.7	7.9
United Kingdom	13.5	7.9
Germany	59.2	45.7
France	6.8	8.9
Italy	24.0	18.5
Belgium	37.1	33.4
Holland	54.9	45.6
Switzerland	54.1	39.9
Japan	12.0	6.5

Notes:
– External reserve ratios: external reserves at the year end as a percentage of the stock of domestic liquid assets.
– The liquid assets include, in this table, only the stock of money as such. *Source: International Financial Statistics.*
– The figures are for the positions at the end of December, 1958 and the last available for 1968, which vary according to the country.

facts must be kept in mind. First, the reserves may be very quickly lost, whereas the adjustment process, it may be assumed, would take some time before having an effect on the balance of payments. Second, we certainly should not exclude the likelihood that monetary authorities will proceed to a compensatory creation of money: I have not seen *any* country since the end of the war which has not been led to offset—to some extent at least—the deflationary effect of a foreign deficit by means of expanding domestic credit. It could not be said they were entirely wrong: a sudden deficit of some importance in the balance of payments is likely to have an unbearable deflationary effect if it was to result in a positive *decline* in the stock of money. An adjustment process of such violence—particularly if it was started by speculative capital flows—would be politically intolerable in almost all countries. This is the reason why at least partial compensation is necessary—as a kind of shock-absorber—but this is also the reason why reserve ratios of 6 to 8 per cent are far too low for countries heavily involved in international transactions.

Reserve ratios of the other countries listed in the table are clearly much higher, Italy being in an intermediate position. But it should be strongly emphasized that apart from Germany, the other countries (Belgium, Holland and Switzerland) are relatively small. This implies that if reserves were distributed evenly between all the countries in the table, the position of the four large countries suffering from an obvious shortage would be only partially improved at the expense of seriously deteriorating the position of the more fortunate countries, including Germany. The total external reserves of the nine countries represent only 15 per cent of their stock of money at the end of 1968, whereas the reserve ratio was 24 per cent ten years previously. Is this not the definition of an *international* shortage of liquidity?

These conclusions are strengthened if the stock of quasi-money was to be included in the denominator of our ratio. The result is given in Table II/b which needs no detailed comment. It reflects the well-known fact that near-money assets have grown much faster over the last ten years in most countries than currency holdings and sight deposits. Of course, these assets could not leave a country without triggering off a violent adjustment process. But it is precisely *for this reason* that the monetary authorities will be unable to refuse the compensatory creation

Table II/b

External reserve ratios

	1958	1968
United States	10.9	3.9
United Kingdom	n.a.	n.a.
Germany	28.2	14.3
France	6.5	8.3
Italy	13.9	10.2
Belgium	32.3	24.4
Holland	27.6	17.0
Switzerland	22.6	13.5
Japan	4.2	2.4

Notes:
- The liquid assets include the stock of money as such *and* the stock of quasi-money. *Source:* International Financial Statistics.
- The figures are for the positions at the end of December, 1958 and the last available for 1968, which vary according to the country.

of money: no government is in a position to let financial intermediation break down. The international mobility of liquid domestic financial assets could therefore lead to the disappearance of the exchange reserves of a country well before the adjustment mechanism, operating at a politically acceptable rate, could restore the equilibrium of the external accounts. In order to avoid this, the country concerned would be obliged to introduce exchange controls or take measures which indirectly would achieve the same purpose, even if technically they bore another name. This is precisely what has happened in a growing number of countries since four years.

In conclusion, therefore, it may be said that at least three series of facts point to a shortage of international liquidity. The war of escalation in interest rates, the generalization of exchange controls and/or of regulation of movements of funds across the borders prove the growing concern of governments with the level of their external reserves; the decline of these reserves relative to the volume of domestic liquid assets provides an economic explanation, based on figures, of this government behaviour.

Towards the Dollar Standard?

If the main lines of this reasoning are accepted, one is tempted to believe that the world economy will head not towards an orderly and gradual demonetization of gold but (through repeated crises) either towards the dollar-standard or the generalization of exchange controls, or even probably towards both at the same time. Over the last few months, we have made fast progress in both these directions. I will admit without reticence that, for a number of good or bad reasons, I find this hard to swallow.

The control of capital flows is a strong temptation for *all* governments at present in power: the number of countries which have not put this into practice one way or another may be counted on the tips of the fingers. It has ardent defenders in many circles. Political men refuse to bear the servitude imposed on them by sudden movements of capital: not so long ago a certain Head of State, in a famous speech, stigmatized capital exports in the name of public morality. Tradition is on their side: the Articles of Agreement of the International Monetary Fund and the reports of the debates at the time should be read again to get a clear idea of the net preference given to the liberalization of current transaction over that of capital flows. Many economists claim that the freeing of foreign trade enables us to achieve an optimum allocation of resources *without* factor mobility, thus well justifying political hostility towards free movements of capital. I have even heard some bankers—whose deposits in national currency were attracted by the astronomical rates on the Euro-dollar market—speak of the good old times before 1958 when such things could hardly ever happen.

I don't think these arguments can simply be pushed aside. It is obvious that capital movements have in some instances caused considerable difficulty in the management of the domestic economy, leading to sacrifices in welfare. Tradition and political instincts are not always wrong. It is also true that the demonstration of economic theory of the equalization of factor rewards through international trade is quite convincing. Finally, I do not need to be persuaded that it is not easy to manage a bank in an open economy when your depositors possess daily information on Euro-dollar interest rates. However, when all this is said, a powerful argument may be made against all those who would like to see a return to the system existing before 1958: a general control of capital flows will be *ineffective* without re-introducing restrictions on trade in goods and services.

I gave you earlier two examples of the interconnection between capital flows and current transactions. A study of the different measures taken over two years by several of the large countries shows how easily the control of movements of "pure" capital overflows into that of current transactions. As an example, there was the British surcharge and more recently the deposit of funds in the case of imports. There are also the German measures—for opposite reasons, of course,—involving tax abatement. Then there is the set of American measures which provide us with a text-book case: the subtle definition of capital exports which does not neglect—for good reasons—the non-repatriation of profits made outside the United States, although nobody denies that transfers of profits should be considered for all other purposes as current transactions. Finally, we could consider the precision of the French exchange control which covers all the finer points of the financing of foreign trade.

It is all more interesting to note that, in spite of these steps leading towards the control of current transactions, the measures taken in each of the countries I have just mentioned have proved unsatisfactory. Statistically they succeeded but, for mysterious reasons, there has always been a disappointing compensation in other items of the balance of payments. Exports of capital from the United States fell sharply, due mainly to incoming capital in search of portfolio investments; at the same time, however, the traditional surplus in the trade balance disappeared. In spite of the success of the British exchange control, the overseas trade figures did not respond to economic policy. The French exchange control appears to be exceptionally efficient but, for reasons unknown to me, the French trade balance is still in the red; in fact, it has deteriorated. The Germans, in their turn, managed to export considerable amounts of capital in 1967 and 1968 but the surplus from their current account reached an all-time high during the same years.

I am convinced that part of the explanation lies in the fact that the statistical definition of the current transactions is unsatisfactory, as it is inevitable that with the ever growing volume and redoubtable complexity of foreign trade and thanks to man's inventive genius, much capital flows through the channels provided for movements of goods and services. Furthermore, those capital funds, which are unable to do so directly, will do it indirectly, by means of an adjustment mechanism which proves the golden rule of macro-economic analysis, according to which the balance of payments forms a *unity* which can only be cut up into pieces where there is a general control of all transactions. Only such a control could prevent changes in one component of the balance of payments to be offset by compensating changes in some other components.

The other alternative, the dollar-standard, merits criticism for fundamental political reasons. Contrary to what has just been said regarding the control of movements of capital, this alternative is by no means impossible. On the contrary, it seems highly practicable, at least technically. The power, organization and innovating capacity of the American industry make such a formidable competitor for the rest of the world that the latter could hardly accept a devaluation of the dollar relatively to all the other currencies. If the dollar was to lose its gold parity, the large majority of countries would be obliged to follow the dollar in order to protect their competitive position.

This, of course, has been known to us for some time. Until about a year ago, however, such a dollar standard could not have been established without at least some reaction from the rest of the world. This reaction might have taken the form of regional groupings, the establishment of regional currencies or monetary areas, involving—admittedly —the risk of increased regional protectionism. While many of us would have regretted a return to protectionism, there would have remained at least some balance of power in the world economy and this would have implied the possibility of negotiation and discussions.

I do not think that this possibility is any longer open to us. The political troubles in various European countries, coupled with the weakening of the currency of one of the main European countries and the emergence of balance-of-payments deficits in others would make it rather difficult to form a "countervailing" monetary power in Europe. Therefore there are practically no obstacles in the way of the dollar standard.

Recent market trends confirm this opinion: there has been no weakening of the dollar on the foreign exchange markets when the very poor balance-of-payments figures were announced for the United States in May. I do not think that this can be explained away by the high interest rates on dollar deposits. There seems to be the recognition that while the U.S. economy may have to face serious inflationary disturbances, no other countries are immune to these, and that, on balance, it is safer, or at least as safe, to hold dollars as any other currency, with the possible exception of the DMark.

However, we must be aware of the most serious implications of the kind of demonetization of gold which would be implied by the dollar standard. We can have a mild foretaste of these political reactions by reading the European press on the "war of escalation" in interest rates, triggered off by U.S. borrowings on the Euro-dollar market, which is regarded as the main culprit in the financing problems encountered in many European countries. The dollar standard implies that the world outside the United States loses all independence in economic policy. We would have to adopt the rate of inflation (or deflation) chosen by the American economy. I am lacking the courage to outline the political consequences of such a loss of economic sovereignty in face of the United States: they are bound to be disastrous, for the United States itself as well as for the rest of the world.

The way out

To sum up the main line of argument developed on the preceding pages. We can only hope to achieve the progressive de-monetization of gold if we succeed in improving the adjustment process and if we manage to ensure, in an orderly way, the growth of international liquidity. In fact, we have seen that the process of adjustment is unlikely to become more effective by itself and that there are signs of shortage of international liquidity. We are thus moving towards repeated crises with the likely consequences that the little remaining freedom in international transactions will be abandoned and that we will adopt (implicitly) the dollar standard. If we want to avoid this, we will have to deal with the root of the problem, i.e. both with the adjustment process and with the inadequate creation of international liquidity.

On this second problem, there is some hope now. The mechanics of special drawing rights is a substantial step in the right direction and follows the logics of the demonetization of gold. This would be a useful, flexible and rational way of creating reserves. It ought to be put in function as quickly as possible.

One must add, however, immediately that we would never be able to create adequate reserves if there was no substantial improvement in the adqustment process. The need for reserves increase indefinitely when the mechanics of adjustment breaks down. Here we come to the inevitable conclusion that exchange rates will have to become more flexible, if we are to avoid persistent deficit or surplus positions in international payments. We cannot expect governments to give up their desire (and duty) to pursue in their economic policy objectives; we have no reason to expect that in the future spending decisions will react more speedily to policy measures than in the past; and finally I fail to see how we could control efficiently capital movements without putting a brake on international trade of goods and services. This leaves us with no alternative: only changes in exchange rate—*any* type of changes—can speed up sufficiently the creaking adjustment process.

This is not a very original conclusion. Since the late nineteen-thirties, we have been teaching in our universities that there is an incompatibility between rigidly pegged exchange rates, the freedom of international transactions and the simultaneous achievement of domestic and external balance. Unless we are exceptionally lucky, something must give way: I hope that this will be the rigidity of exchange rates. The experience of the last two years tends to suggest that after all economic theory is perhaps not a meaningless exercise.

June, 1969

COMMENTARIES

Following the presentation of his paper by Professor Lamfalussy, the President of the Foundation called upon each member of the panel in turn for comment.

Wilfrid Baumgartner:

May I say first how pleased I am to have this excellent opportunity, thanks to Ambassador Burgess and the Jacobsson Foundation, to meet so many old friends and so many old problems, too.

I remember the last words of a Marilyn Monroe film, where the final sentence was: "Nobody is perfect." May I say in respect to Professor Lamfalussy's paper, that it was perfect. I have rarely read and heard so intelligent an analysis of the present monetary situation in the world.

I should like to begin by saying that I was never a fetishist of gold. I remember refusing to follow the line indicated to me years ago, before the war, by my predecessor in a public agency. He said to me: "One thing is certain, young man, one thing is certain: a banker should never grant any credit." He had some excuse, since it was just after the difficult period of the economic crisis of the early thirties; it is obvious, however, that it is normally better to follow a different course.

I also remember a British friend who used to explain to me, every time I met him, that he saw no essential difference between the mines of South Africa and the vaults of the central banks. More recently, it has been possible, in my country, to draw a parallel between damage caused to the French financial situation and speeches made about the price of gold. These speeches have each been good incentives to further hoarding of gold, which was certainly not to the advantage or interest of the French economy and of Frenchmen themselves. I should therefore be prepared, in principle, to sympathize with Professor Lamfalussy's position, when he says—if I am correctly interpreting his train of thought—that he is not basically an adversary of the demonetization of gold. In my opinion, the problem is knowing whether such a demonetization is possible; to be quite frank, I would doubt it at the present time. Professor Lamfalussy has explained the declining role of gold in what is called the international monetary system. This trend certainly exists, but it began a long time ago. Even in the time of the so-called gold standard, the role of international credit was already very important and I have sometimes thought, I must say, that gold, which was chosen as a standard because of its rarity, may become obsolete in the future because of the same rarity, in view of world needs for liquidity. Nevertheless, it was chosen as a basis and has been maintained as a basis and as such, in my opinion, it is still useful; but it is precisely for this reason that one cannot talk of gold prices in the same way as one talks of other prices.

Monetary policy is not an end in itself. It must contribute to a rational economic development and a progressive improvement of the standard of living for all people and in all countries, many of which do not maintain gold reserves.

The main difficulty is the one which Professor Lamfalussy underlined so neatly: the problem of the adjustment process, as well as that of the amount of world liquidity. The latter is obviously the easier of the two problems to solve. The proposals made by the International Monetary Fund concerning Special Drawing Rights have appeared to me to be logical and adequate and I am personally satisfied with the approval which almost all governments have now given them. I have always been confident in the management of the Fund; it was this confidence which led me to participate, eight years ago, with Per Jacobsson and some of my friends, both American and European, in the creation of the Group of Ten. In my opinion, the amount of monetary reserves can presently be more adequately realized through SDR's than through a change in the price of gold. I was delighted, two weeks ago, to hear my successor in the French Treasury saying that he was not at all interested in a modification of the price of gold.

With regard to the problem of the adjustment process, the recent adjustment in France was of the kind which is tolerated by the Fund on the grounds that it is better to use surgery than medicine. As far as medicine is concerned, I am not really prepared to support the idea of more flexible rates for currencies. I still believe—and this is not simply the reaction of the industrialist which I have become—that fixed parities continue to be the best solution for the whole world.

Maybe it would be possible to enlarge a little what used to be called the gold points but, in my opinion, no more than that.

I do not believe that anything can be said on the problem of the adjustment process—which is obviously linked with the problem of world liquidity—that would be more logical than the view expressed in the last report of the B.I.S.:

"It cannot be said too often that no international monetary system will work properly unless countries are prepared to follow domestic policies that are compatible with the maintenance of external equilibrium. The task of monetary cooperation and coordination is to operate in a way that assists countries in achieving this essential goal."(*)

My only reservation on this text is that it appears to speak only of monetary authorities, and yet the process of adjustment is certainly primarily a problem for governments.

It is my hope that, in the future, monetary difficulties can be met by the application of two magic worlds: for internal policies, "seriousness"; and for international policy, "cooperation."

Guido Carli:

We must be especially grateful to Professor Lamfalussy for the extremely stimulating paper which he has submitted to us. I greatly welcome the opportunity to take part in this discussion as, on the whole, I share his economic policy preferences and his method of approaching this problem.

The economic policy preferences which I would like to see realized in the medium-term are, stated simply, "gradual demonetization of gold and its replacement by an international monetary reserve asset."

Like Professor Lamfalussy, I am deeply concerned about the serious dangers entailed in an alternative solution involving the replacing of gold with a national currency, and in particular, about the risks inherent in a situation which would give rise to a "dollar standard."

*Bank for International Settlements, *Thirty-Ninth Annual Report*, Basle, 9th June 1969. Page 184.

Should the United States decide to cut the link between the dollar and gold—i.e., to stop buying and selling gold at a fixed price—the trading partners of the United States would have the following possibilities:

—to allow the dollar to fluctuate on their markets;

—to tie their currencies to the dollar at a fixed parity, which would force them either to follow a monetary and financial policy similar to that of the United States or to accumulate an unlimited amount of dollars should they become creditors, or to depend on U.S. credits should they become debtors;

—to maintain a fixed parity vis-a-vis the dollar for commercial transactions, but to allow the dollar to fluctuate freely for financial transactions, as the Swiss authorities did after the Second World War.

The advocates of the "dollar standard" believe that, especially when the relatively small influence of the foreign component on the United States GNP is considered, such a solution would not only be in the interest of the United States but would also resolve the complex problems inherent in the adjustment of the disequilibria between the American and the European areas, the latter being an EEC enlarged to include the United Kingdom and the Scandinavian countries. I am not against limited flexibility of exchange rates between large monetary areas where such flexibility proves to be necessary to complete the adjustment process when demand management policies, even if successful in re-establishing internal stability, are incapable of achieving external adjustment. Nevertheless, I am not indifferent to the dangers of unlimited flexibility between monetary blocs as a result of a unilateral decision of the United States.

Should such a decision be taken, the reactions might be much more complex than those foreseen by the supporters of the dollar standard. First of all, the currencies of the EEC countries would fluctuate among themselves to the extent that the policies adopted by the individual EEC member countries differed. As a result, the process of economic integration presently under way would come to a stop and subsequently give way to the breakdown of the Community. Another result might be the introduction of fixed par values vis-a-vis the dollar for the settlement of current transactions, while the so-called "financial dollar" would fluctuate. However, a system like this, which presupposes the introduction of exchange controls, would soon be followed by the adoption of quotas and of other quantitative restrictions which would ultimately restrain the competitiveness of American goods on other markets. In fact, this would lead to a long period of monetary disorder, characterized by unstable exchange rates and the spreading of administrative controls on the movements of goods, persons, and capital, after which it would be necessary to return to a system of fixed parities.

The dangers of a dollar standard unilaterally imposed by the United States are therefore quite evident. Moreover, it is difficult to believe that a similar standard could be introduced by an international agreement under which member countries of the international community would be allowed to interfere in the shaping of the financial and monetary policies of the United States.

If we take into account the various components of world reserves and try to determine what is in store for each of them in the future, we cannot but reach the following conclusions:

(a) As regards gold, not only will its proportion in total reserves gradually diminish, but it will be used less and less for settlement of international transactions. At the present time, gold-holding countries behave practically as if gold did not exist. In the event of a balance of payments deficit, they first resort to their foreign exchange reserves and then to swaps, or to their reserve position in the Fund if they have any. Gold is sold practically as a last resort, that is, when all or nearly all the credit tranche has been used. Alternatively, countries in a surplus position accumulate dollars, activate swaps to help debtor countries, add to their reserve positions in the Fund, and extend medium-term credit denominated in national currencies. Only as a last possibility are they able to increase their gold reserves. Paradoxically, gold has become the least liquid component of reserves. The Washington agreement on the two-tier gold market, the success of which is hardly questionable, has quite clearly created a distinction between monetary and non-monetary gold. If, as I hope, this agreement will continue to be the basis of gold policy of major industrial countries, monetary gold would change as a consequence only of decisions to be taken by the IMF, and not of the vagaries of gold production. The metal would serve mainly to satisfy the growing needs of industry and the demand of hoarders. The price of gold on the free market might still, for some time, be affected by the conventional price of $35 per ounce for official transactions. However, in the long run, it will have to depend entirely on market forces.

(b) As far as major trading currencies are concerned, we still witness a gradual reduction of their use as reserve assets.

The pound sterling has practically ceased to be used as a reserve asset since last year's Basle arrangements, when the major industrial countries agreed to finance fluctuations in the sterling holdings of the Sterling Area countries. The latter countries tend increasingly to diversify the composition of their reserves by including new assets such as the dollar and gold. The French franc is following a somewhat similar pattern, though on a smaller scale because of its less important international role.

As far as the United States dollar is concerned, although it is increasingly used in the settlement of international commercial and financial transactions it is used less and less as a reserve asset. Indeed, there is an increasing tendency for central banks to maintain in their reserves a sufficient volume of dollars to intervene on the exchange markets. (In particular, we may perceive an evolution by which the dollar will continue to be used as an intervention asset on the exchange markets and for the settlement of commercial and financial transactions, but progressively less as a reserve asset.)

(c) Another reserve asset, which has been used more and more in the last few years, is a member's credit position in the Fund, that is, the position resulting from the gold subscription and the use by the Fund of the member's currency to finance external deficits. We are, in fact, referring to the so-called "gold and super gold tranche positions" which have practically tripled in the last decade without, however, exceeding 10 per cent of total reserves.

As this reserve component is nothing but a by-product of the financing of external deficits, and does not necessarily correspond to the needs of the system, we cannot expect an adequate contribution to the needs of international liquidity from this source. In all likelihood, this component will continue to play a marginal role.

In my opinion, a rational setup of the international monetary system should include the following features:

(a) *Special Drawing Rights,* which are about to be activated for the first time, seem to be destined to become, within ten or fifteen years, the main component of world reserves. For this to take place it is necessary not only that they be created in amounts corresponding to the needs of the system and in accordance with the correct working of the adjustment process, but that they be judiciously spent by countries, i.e., much in the same way as they would spend their first line reserves. It is likely that some time in the course of this process it will be necessary to eliminate the absolute gold guarantee which presently characterizes SDRs;

(b) to the extent that Special Drawing Rights will gradually assert themselves as the most important component of world reserves, the volume of *monetary gold* will in all probability tend to decrease.

(c) *National currencies,* especially *dollars* (but sterling and French francs too for countries in the respective monetary areas) will be maintained in the reserves in limited amounts to serve as intervention currencies.

(d) *Reserve Positions* in the Fund will continue to carry moderate weight in world reserves. They are the counterpart of the monetary financing of external disequilibria and can be assimilated to the accumulation of dollars and sterling, but with the difference that they are an international asset rather than national currencies;

(e) furthermore, in a second line position, there will continue to be some components in the reserves which, however transient, are presently considered to be indispensable for the good functioning of the system. I am referring to Reciprocal Monetary Agreements presently existing with the Federal Reserve Bank of New York. They are an assurance to central banks that they will have at their disposal at any time the cash which is needed for the financing of their essential interventions on the exchange markets;

(f) finally, credits denominated in national currencies, with a maturity of more than one year and with a clause providing for their mobilization, will continue to be included in the official medium term foreign position of the monetary authorities.

The problems which will arise in the transitional period between the present moment and the final elimination of gold from the system are of great importance. Although I am convinced that the demonetization of the metal constitutes the rational final solution, I cannot overlook the fact that gold is presently the main component of reserves and that, therefore, central bankers have an interest in avoiding a decrease in its price.

In my view, for the transitional period to unfold smoothly it would be desirable:

(a) that the IMF commit itself to buy monetary gold (that is the gold existing in world reserves on the eve of the Washington agreement or other date to be agreed upon) without quantitative limitations at $35 per ounce, to be paid in national currencies or SDRs;

(b) that an agreement be reached among the monetary authorities of the main industrial countries to insure the coexistence of gold with the other reserve assets. It is possible that in a period in which gold continues to be part of the system, yet available only in a limited quantity vis-a-vis demand, competition for gold between central banks might develop. To cope with such an event, Italy has in the past advocated a policy of reserve harmonization along the following rather simple lines:

(i) countries accumulating reserves should receive gold if the ratio of their gold to their total reserves is lower than the ratio of total gold to the total reserves of the countries belonging to the agreement;

(ii) countries losing reserves should sell gold if the ratio of their gold to their total reserves is higher than the ratio of total gold to the total reserves of this group of countries. In the opposite case, they should give up other assets.

More sophisticated versions of a policy of reserve harmonization have been advocated by well-known economists, such as Triffin, Bernstein, etc., the main idea of their various proposals being that gold would be deposited, possibly with other assets, in "settlement accounts" to be opened with international monetary institutions which, in turn, would issue certificates that could be used in official settlements.

Whilst formulating solutions for the transitional period, we are fully aware that public opinion continues to attribute intrinsic value to monetary gold. We may express amusement at this conviction, but as politicians or central bankers we cannot ignore it. Good use must be made of the transitional period to inform, in a simple but effective way, public opinion and so finally to destroy the "golden calf".

I believe I can agree in general with Professor Lamfalussy in the view that, for the demonetization of gold to take place, the necessary conditions are, on the one hand, a proper creation of unconditional liquidity through the SDR mechanism and on the other hand, the satisfactory working of the adjustment process. I also agree with him that should the latter condition not materialize, it would be most difficult to continue deliberately to create international liquidity.

The satisfactory working of the adjustment process might require the introduction of two changes in the international monetary system.

First, the creation of a mechanism for the recycling of wandering capital. The growing volume of financial assets, both liquid and semi-liquid, the businessman's greater ingenuity, the refinement of the financial instruments used, the existence of multinational corporations managing their liquid assets and their sources of financing with centralized criteria, and the possibility of anticipating or postponing payments for such a period of time that would involve the use of large sums, all increase the risk of large shifts of funds from one market to another. This is the price we are paying in advancing towards a more integrated world economy. Nevertheless, as we saw in November 1968, May 1969, and recently, capital movements from one market to another can be too large for the available reserves and international credit to finance them. During past months, I contributed to formulating the scheme which is known as "recycling". The perplexity and skepticism with which these suggestions were received are to be explained by the reluctance of the monetary authorities of the countries concerned to commit themselves to an automatic or semi-automatic recycling without the guarantee of a much closer coordination of their economic policies. In this respect we have to recognize that in the determination of medium-term objectives (balance of payments, growth, prices, and so on), international cooperation has not made much progress. Even the principle contained in the EEC Treaties that the determination of exchange rates is a matter of common interest has remained practically a dead letter. In other words, while integration of national economies is rapidly progressing at the corporate level, both private and public, the instruments of international cooperation are lagging far behind the needs which this integration has created. Nevertheless, in an international context such as this, where capital moves across national boundaries with much the same intensity and magnitude as within one country, a recycling mechanism is absolutely necessary; otherwise, the very foundations on which the smooth working of the system is based would disintegrate. This is one of the problems on which governments should focus their attention.

Second, we cannot be unaware of the difficulties encountered by governments in changing par values, when par values seem inappropriate with respect to the maintenance of sustainable external equilibrium and internal stability. It will probably be impossible to overcome these difficulties, as a change in par values will always be of advantage to some groups and of disadvantage to others. In order for the system to work smoothly, a useful change might be to introduce greater flexibility in external monetary relations by using the co-called crawling peg. This problem is being studied by the staffs of international monetary institutions, and central banks are now reflecting on it. Additional thought will be necessary, not only as regards the working of the mechanism (which lies in the possibility of small changes, for instance 2 per cent per year, of par values in accordance with the market behaviour during a certain time), but also as regards the economic effects. A 2 per cent per year crawling peg, for instance, does not mean the introduction of flexible exchange rates, nor necessarily the widening of the present margins in which rates are allowed to fluctuate. It is in fact compatible with stable exchange rates. These rates would continue to vary within extremely narrow limits around a point of reference—i.e., the par value —which may be slightly modified every year in the light of market indications. I do not think that such a system would be detrimental to the smooth working of the EEC. On the contrary, small annual adjustments of par values, to compensate for divergent price trends which result from insufficient coordination of aims and economic policies would, in my opinion, be preferable to large variations, which usually occur under the pressure of external events.

In concluding these comments I would like to express my confidence that the final disappearance of gold as a monetary asset within the next ten to fifteen years will make a remarkable contribution to the strengthening of international monetary cooperation. All Fund member countries will then have to determine in common the amount of liquidity to be created and no longer leave it to events which are beyond their responsible control.

L. K. Jha:

Mr. Chairman, I am glad that you reminded me and all of us that what we are discussing really is the role of gold, and not the international monetary system or the possible changes in the working of that system toward a more viable and a better balanced world.

I noticed that Mr. Lamfalussy, who had given us an excellent paper, which he has followed up by an equally excellent address, had some difference in emphasis between his paper and his verbal presentation. In his paper he had gone all out for demonetization of gold as the answer to the present problems of the world. In his oral presentation he emphasized more particularly the importance of making the adjustment process work better. Between these two positions I feel that there is a link which should be there, but is missing. The question is: are we satisfied that, but for gold, the adjustment process would work better? On that question I do not think we have had a positive presentation which would carry conviction. Professor Lamfalussy's paper very rightly drew attention to two problems: one, the problem of liquidity, in which context the constraint of gold was obvious; and, two, the desirability of getting away from gold as far as possible in order to improve the basis of world liquidity beyond any question of doubt. On this latter, when expounding the importance of making the adjustment process work, Professor Lambalussy did not provide, nor has he done so this afternoon, reasons to make us feel confident that, if only we could get rid of this villain gold, governments will do the right things, either in the matter of par values or in the matter of domestic policies or in respect of international capital movements.

As to the public superstition about the importance of gold, we, as experts and central bankers and economists, can afford to scoff at it. However, insofar as this sentiment persists, I do suggest that it does and can operate helpfully toward bringing about the needed adjustment. When a country starts losing gold, or is about to lose gold, some things happen. Public opinion does become responsive to the need for a change. That change could be either in the par value of the currency or in domestic policies. There is at such a time a certain consciousness, a certain realization which pervades the public mind in a more dramatic, more positive way. Therefore, when we get away from the problem of liquidity and look at the problem of adjustment, the link with gold still serves a valuable end.

In saying this, I am not for a moment suggesting that we should, as a matter of policy or of long-term objective, continue to live under the tyranny of gold. Emotionally as well as intellectually, I agree that we must try to get away from gold and to find other satisfactory reserve assets. But when we are discussing the role of gold, in the next decade —and that is the period suggested as our term of reference—we have to take a more careful view on whether it is practicable, or even desirable, within the next decade, to think in terms of demonetization as a possible answer.

The speakers before me have ruled out, and rightly, the idea that the world might adopt the dollar standard. This suggestion raises problems, not only for other countries, but even for the United States. Without going into those details, I should say, we have to recognize that gold is the one form of reserve asset which does not immediately constitute somebody else's liability. Problems arise whenever the reserves of one country or a group of countries are the liabilities for the countries whose currencies are being so held. That is a situation in which, some time or other, sooner or later, you are apt to run into serious difficulties. This is why it is not right to think in terms of any currency, the dollar or any other, being the standard the rest of the world should adopt. If there is to be a new standard, it will have to be on the lines of the SDRs; that is, it will have to have an international backing.

It would be dangerous if, at this juncture, when we are about to bring the SDR system into being, we were to overload it with suggestions or nuances that the system is being planned as one of pure paper money.

It may become so in course of time. I hope it will. But at this moment, in our immediate projections, we must be very firm in standing by the view that it is a means of adding to liquidity; it is, up to a point, a substitute for gold, but it is not a replacement for gold in the ultimate sense in the immediately foreseeable and predictable future. That, I think, is the way we can create greater confidence in SDRs. It is, to my mind, wrong to speak of demonetisation of gold at this stage and the adoption by implication, of a pure paper currency for international use.

We have certainly made good progress in reducing the dependence on or subservience to gold. The market price is now different from the official price and the two markets are segregated. When this two-tier system came to be introduced, we in India felt rather like the character in Moliere's play who had been talking prose all his life without knowing that he was doing so. We have had a two-tier system for gold in practice in India for many years. No one in India, not even a Treasury official or central banker, could really tell you straightaway what the official price of gold is in rupees. He would start with $35 an ounce, multiply it by the prevailing rate of exchange, and then work out the rupee price. There is no mystique, no sanctity in the idea of the rupee having a certain par value in gold. If the market price of gold goes up or down, we take much less notice of it than we would take of the price of rice or wheat going up or down. This, I am inclined to think, is perhaps a reasonable reaction such as we may all one day have in regard to the gold price. But, the fact remains that the decision on the two-tier system produced great excitement. Some thought it was a calamity. Attempts were made to arrest a rise in free market prices, and, in the process, if I may say so, somewhat indefensible positions were taken. We said we would not buy gold even at $35. One could understand the decision to plug the outflows of gold from the monetary system into open market. But to take at the same time the line that there should be no inflow either, did not seem to me to be very logical. I do appreciate that we cannot accept a position in which gold producers will treat us, central bankers and the monetary system, in the same way as farmers treat the support authorities for commodity prices. When prices sag, they come to us, but when they rise they wish to sell to the free market. In these matters, there has to be a two-way obligation.

I do feel it is sensible and, indeed, highly essential for us to economize the use of gold. We should assume in that context a problem that will arise shortly, namely, the demand for gold in connection with the increases in quotas in the Fund. Mr. Schweitzer will be asking us all to give him gold. Now, if this gold exercise is not going to be a matter of robbing Pierre to pay Paul, we shall have to think whether this is an occasion when the monetary system should increase its holding of gold or whether some alternative to this is feasible. This is a practical question we must soon face. If not, we could only have a reshuffle of some holdings, followed by some draft on the U.S., and some mitigation by the IMF. The solution will have to be planned; or, else, we will not quite know what we have exactly done or achieved.

So, Mr. Chairman, after listening to all that has been said today and as a result of the thinking that I have done on the problem, my view on the future of gold is this: that the time has not come when we can dethrone gold. What we can do and should do is to turn him into a constitutional monarch, who must set his seal of approval on any piece of paper that his Prime Minister to my right, the Managing Director of the IMF, presents to him, with the full concurrence of the Board of Governors.

QUESTIONS AND ANSWERS

During the course of the earlier statements, a number of written questions were submitted by members of the audience. These were given to the various speakers for answering; in addition, Professor Lamfalussy was given the opportunity to comment on the remarks made by other members of the panel.

Professor Lamfalussy:

I may perhaps begin by saying two words about what Mr. Baumgartner said. I think our views are very similar, with one exception which I believe to be fairly essential.

I do think that we have to co-ordinate policies. I also think that national governments have to carry the responsibility of implementing appropriate policies. But my point is that there are circumstances under which these policies simply cannot be carried out in an appropriate way.

In order to achieve external balance, we ought to be able, in principle, to synchronize the rates of increases in prices. Now, the rate of increase in prices is governed by many factors, some of which cannot be brought under the control of government policy. This is why we must leave to governments some—and in a few cases a large—degree of freedom policies. *All* policies cannot be co-ordinated or harmonized. Hence my insistence on exchange rate adjustment.

As regards Governor Carli, I am entirely in agreement with what he has said, including his last very precise definition of the type of exchange rate changes that he would favour.

Governor Jha, I think, is entirely right in reminding me that there might have been a misunderstanding in what I said. If the misunderstanding is really there, I must correct it. I did not want to say and I do not want to say that if only we could get rid of gold, we would have a better adjustment process. I think there is no link between these two things this way. What I was trying to say is that, *if* we want to get rid of gold for a number of reasons, which I did not state but which are to a very large extent political or emotional— but these can be nevertheless very respectable reasons—if we want to get rid of gold, *then* we must have a substantial improvement in the adjustment process. I think the relation goes this way and not the other way around.

Now, here I have a certain number of questions.

Question No. 1: *Why did the speculators think early in 1968 that the dollar price of gold was likely to rise?* Well, I could facetiously reply that I do not know, because I was not among them; but this is perhaps too easy an answer. I think the answer is because they expected that the two-tier system would not work and that, sooner or later, there would be purchases by the central banks. I think the underlying strength of the private gold market is potential demand from central banks. If really everybody was persuaded that the central banks would not come into that market forever, then I think very likely that the gold price would fall, and the fact that the gold price is still above $35 proves precisely that people do not believe that the central banks will forever refrain from purchasing gold.

Question No. 2: *The preference for gold and its growing scarcity will create a problem of qualitative liquidity in a multiple reserve system. Do you recognize the existence of that problem and how do you propose to solve it?* I think this is a real problem and I certainly do recognize its existence. As regards the Special Drawing Rights, so long as they are gold-guaranteed, the qualitative problem hopefully will not exist. As for the national currencies which are part of international reserves, the qualitative problem may arise, especially when the reserve currency's country experiences a rate of inflation which is judged to be higher than the rate of inflation elsewhere. I think, on the other hand, that so long as the problem of inflation does not exist, I would not regard the quality problem as a very substantial one within the present institutional framework.

Question No. 3 is a very curious question: *If there is persistent inflationary pressure, wouldn't private firms find it efficient to use gold as a means of payment and reserve, thus assuring a continued monetary role to gold, whatever central banks may do?* Well, I think there is probably a case where this might happen. If inflation really got entirely out of hand over the world, and we had galloping inflation of the kind some countries had in the twenties, this sort of thing might happen, just as in some countries after the war, cigarettes became really money. In this case, gold can become a means of payment and reserve, but, short of this extreme hypothesis, I simply don't see how this could happen. There are no interest payments on gold. Moreover, experience in most countries has shown that gold has not been a profitable investment over time, and since firms are supposed to be managed on the basis of profit maximization, I doubt that they would really invest much in gold.

The next question: *Is the chronic monetary crisis not the result of what you call the decline in the monetary function of gold, due to the lack of gold liquidity and to lack of convertibility of the dollar into gold?* It is certainly right, I think, to say that we would not have had the same type of crisis as we had in March 1968, had there been an absolutely clear gold guarantee to the dollar, but I think the March 1968 crisis was a rather peculiar one and the crises we have had since then belong to a different kind of family.

Question No. 5: *Is there not a danger that, with a system of greater flexibility in exchange rates, we get an improvement in the adjustment process at the price of retrogression in economic and financial integration?* I think this really touches the heart of the matter. My answer is no; or at least I do not believe that the kind of retrogression we would get is really worse than the one we would get if we persist in not having a proper adjustment process. Let me spell this out in just two words.

What sort of retrogression can we have with a greater flexibility of exchange rates? I think you can sum it up perhaps in an over-simplified way by saying that in a world of more flexible exchange rates, we, in fact, impose additional costs on international financial and trade transactions. I mean, if traders, industrialists, importers, exporters want to get adequate coverage, they would have to pay for it and the arbitration mechanism will develop in an adequate way. Of course, this protection will cost something and it is through that channel that we will get some negative effect in the amount of international trade or international financial transactions. But I think this is very small in comparison with what we are going to get without an improvement in the adjustment process. We will get controls. In fact, we are already in the midst of many controls on capital flows and we are heading in some cases towards controls on trade and services. I think the social cost and the retrogression on that account is more dangerous than paying something for arbitrage operations, which is not negligible but still a lesser evil.

The final question: *With the international financial system obviously in serious need of change, what in your opinion is the odds that the whole structure will collapse if these changes do not come quickly enough?* I do not think it will collapse. The main reason is that we *did* develop a series of international agreements, measures of co-operation between central banks which certainly did function. In no way did I want to suggest that these measures of co-operation were inefficient. What I was trying to convey is that they cost something because they always added some sort of social cost and/or ended up with controls of some kind. But, given this co-operation and given the various controls we have adopted, I think we can avoid very easily the collapse of the system. But the surviving system will not be a very efficient one.

Governor Jha:

The question is: *What is the future of sterling as a reserve currency?* The answer I would give is along the following lines: For any currency to be a reserve currency, a number of conditions have to be fulfilled. Firstly, its value should be recognized to be stable over a long period of time; secondly, it should have a position in which other countries can acquire its currency and hold it without imparting a sense of weakness in that currency.

At one time sterling did perform this function. I doubt if, in that fundamental sense, it can regain that position. The tendency in all countries which hold sterling is to diversify their reserves as a kind of spread of possible risks, and then to spread it in a manner in which their trading conditions indicate as being the most helpful.

The attempt made last year with the agreement at Basle and the agreement between Britain and the sterling area countries is itself a recognition that sterling is now a reserve currency in a very different sense from what it used to be in the days when the sterling area came into being. This change which has taken place is itself so fundamental that I cannot but conclude that the prospect of returning to the old position is just not there, and it is not even desirable from anyone's point of view to think of harking back to that kind of situation.

QUESTIONS AND ANSWERS — MR. SCHWEITZER

Mr. Schweitzer:

The question is: *Would you please outline the new mechanism or process of international adjustment under the SDR system, and how the burden of adjustment might not necessarily be fully borne by the underdeveloped or capital-importing countries? What would impose a brake or limiting force on inordinate monetary expansion under the SDR's or, in other words, offset the inflationary bias of SDR creation?* We do not feel that the SDR creation has an inflationary bias. We feel that once one had agreed, and I think everybody now has agreed, that there should be a way to increase international liquidity in any kind of rational manner, then to do it through SDR's is the least inflationary one. Just think of the two other means which would be available: doubling the price of gold, which would immediately create $40 billion of internationally expendable purchasing power when we have had quite a lot of discussion about whether $3 billion a year was not too much.

The other method would be to go along with a continuing U.S. deficit on an official settlement basis, assuming the willingness of central bankers to hold unlimited increasing amounts of dollars.

If you compare SDRs to any other ways of increasing international liquidity, this is obviously the way where there is the least inflationary bias. Also one must not think of SDRs as creating some kind of windfall profit which should be spent as soon as it is cashed in. SDRs are supposed to respond to an international need for generally larger reserves, not to create an additional international demand.

In this way, we consider that additional SDRs will facilitate the adjustment process by the fact that there is international liquidity created in reasonable amounts. It will allow the adjustment process to function.

What do we have to achieve presently? The United States has to achieve a reasonable current balance of payments position. The United Kingdom has to run a permanent surplus for quite a long time to come. Many countries, major countries have, I think, very legitimately decided either to reconstitute or to increase their reserves. Developing countries, as far as we can judge their attitude, and you know them very well, feel as a whole a very strong need to increase their reserves. All these aspirations, which have to be achieved through a proper adjustment process, could not possibly be fulfilled at the same time, if there were not some kind of leeway. Otherwise, as Governor Jha said, you could only do it for Pierre by robbing Paul. Then mainly the developing countries would be the victims if you had a real fight amongst all countries to get a larger share of an existing cake. It does not need much imagination to think that the weakest and poorest would be the first victim.

Ambassador Burgess:

I think that pretty well covers the questions that have been asked—not every individual question but the subject matter of all the questions.

If there is no member of the panel who wants to say anything, may I, then, on behalf, I am sure, of you all express our very warm appreciation to all those who have spoken to us today. It has been a tremendous afternoon, with a very fine paper presented and a very good analysis in the commentaries. I think we can adjourn this meeting with an expression of satisfaction for the speakers and for the audience. The ripples of what has been said at this meeting will go out very far. Thank you very much for meeting with us today.

Appendix 1

BIOGRAPHIES

Alexandre Lamfalussy, author of the main paper for this meeting, was born in 1929 in Hungary, studied economics in Belgium and at Nuffield College, Oxford, where he worked for a D.Phil degree. He is now Managing Director of the Banque de Bruxelles, as well as Professor at the University of Louvain. He has written and lectured widely in Europe and the United States (he was Visiting Professor at Yale University during 1961-62), recent titles including the "The U.K. and the Six", "The $35 Question" and "Les marchés financiers en Europe". He is married and lives in Belgium.

Wilfrid Baumgartner, President of Rhone-Poulenc S.A. since 1963, has occupied many posts in the financial field in the French Government. He was Governor of the Bank of France from 1949-1960, Minister of Finance and of Economic Affairs in the Debré Cabinet thereafter and, earlier, held a variety of positions having to do with the management of the financial aspects of the economy. He has also found time to be a Professor at the Ecole Libre des Sciences Politiques and later at the Institut d'Etudes Politiques of Paris. Mr. Baumgartner was born in 1902, is married and lives in Paris. He is an Inspecteur General des Finances Honoraire and holds the honor of Grand Officier of the Légion d'Honneur.

Guido Carli, Governor of the Banca d'Italia, has been concerned with international financial matters for over twenty years. In 1947 he was a member of the first Board of Executive Directors of the International Monetary Fund, being at the same time on the Board of the Italian Foreign Exchange Office, of which he is now Chairman. He was Chairman of the Managing Committee of the European Payments Union, was a member of the Monetary Committee of the European Economic Community and is now on the Board of Directors of the Bank for International Settlements. He was Minister of Foreign Trade in 1957/8 and has been Governor of the Banca d'Italia since 1960. He is also

Governor, for Italy, of the International Bank for Reconstruction and Development and its affiliates, as well as Alternate Governor, for Italy, of the International Monetary Fund. Governor Carli has spoken and written widely on international monetary problems.

L. K. Jha, I.C.S., M.B.E., has been Governor of the Reserve Bank of India since 1967. Prior to that he had been a civil servant with a wide ranging experience in economic administration in India, having been Secretary of the Ministry of Heavy Industries in 1956/57, of the Department of Economic Affairs, Union Finance Ministry in 1960/64, and to the Prime Minister 1964/67. In 1957 he was elected Chairman of the Contracting Parties of GATT, serving through 1958, and was Chairman of the UN Interim Committee for the Coordination of International Committee Arrangements the following two years. He is currently Alternate Governor of the International Monetary Fund for India. Governor Jha, who was born in 1913, graduated from Trinity College, Cambridge, and now lives in Bombay.

Appendix 2

The Per Jacobsson Foundation Sponsors

HONORARY CHAIRMEN

EUGENE R. BLACK *(United States)* former President, International Bank for Reconstruction and Development

MARCUS WALLENBERG *(Sweden)* Chairman, Stockholms Enskilda Bank

CHAIRMAN

W. RANDOLPH BURGESS
(United States) Director, Atlantic Council former United States Ambassador to NATO

HERMAN J. ABS *(Germany)* Chairman, Deutsche Bank A.G.

ROGER AUBOIN *(France)* former General Manager, Bank for International Settlements

WILFRID BAUMGARTNER *(France)* President, Rhone-Poulenc; former Minister of Finance; former Governor, Banque de France

S. CLARK BEISE *(United States)* Chairman of the Executive Committee, Bank of America National Trust and Savings Assn.

B.M. BIRLA *(India)* President, Birla Brothers Private Limited

RUDOLF BRINCKMANN *(Germany)* Partner, Brinckmann, Wirtz & Co.

LORD COBBOLD, P.C. *(United Kingdom)* Lord Chamberlain; former Governor, Bank of England

MIGUEL CUADERNO *(Philippines)* former Governor, Central Bank of the Philippines

R. v. FIEANDT *(Finland)* former Prime Minister; former Governor, Bank of Finland

MAURICE FRERE *(Belgium)* Former Governor, Banque National de Belgique; former President, Bank for International Settlements

E. C. FUSSELL *(New Zealand)* former Governor, Reserve Bank of New Zealand

ALY GRITLY *(United Arab Republic)* former Chairman, Bank of Alexandria

EUGENIO GUDIN *(Brazil)* President, Instituto Brasileiro de Economia, Fundaçao Getulio Vargas; former Minister of Finance

GOTTFRIED HABERLER *(United States)* Professor, Harvard University

VISCOUNT HARCOURT, K.C.M.G., O.B.E. *(United Kingdom)* Managing Director, Morgan Grenfell & Co., Ltd.

GABRIEL HAUGE *(United States)* President, Manufacturers Hanover Trust Co.

CARL OTTO HENRIQUES *

M.W. HOLTROP *(Netherlands)* former President, Bank for International Settlements and De Nederlandsche Bank N.V.

SHIGEO HORIE *(Japan)* Chairman, Committee on International Finance, Federation of Economic Organizations; former Chairman, Bank of Tokyo, Ltd.

CLARENCE E. HUNTER *(United States)* former United States Treasury Representative in Europe

H.V.R. IENGAR *(India)* Chairman, The E.I.D.-Parry Group; former Governor, Reserve Bank of India

KAORU INOUYE *(Japan)* Chairman, Dai Ichi Bank, Ltd.

ALBERT E. JANSSEN *

RAFAELE MATTIOLI *(Italy)* President, Banca Commerciale Italiana

J. J. McELLIGOTT *(Ireland)* former Governor, Central Bank of Ireland

APPENDIX 2

JOHAN MELANDER *(Norway)* Managing Director, Den norske Creditbank

DONATO MENICHELLA *(Italy)* Honorary Governor, Banca d'Italia

EMMANUEL MONICK*(France)* Honorary President, Banque de Paris et des Pays-Bas; former Governor, Banque de France

JEAN MONNET *(France)* President, Action Committee, United States of Europe

WALTER MULLER *(Chile)* former Chilean Ambassador to the United States

JUAN PARDO HEEREN *

FEDERICO PINEDO *(Argentina)* former Minister of Finance

ABDUL QADIR *(Pakistan)* former Governor, State Bank of Pakistan

SVEN RAAB *(Sweden)* Managing Director, Göteborgs Bank

* Deceased

DAVID ROCKEFELLER *(United States)* Chairman of the Board, Chase Manhattan Bank

LORD SALTER, P.C., G.B.E., K.C.B. *(United Kingdom)* former Director, Economic and Financial Section of the League of Nations; former British Government Minister

PIERRE-PAUL SCHWEITZER *(France)* Managing Director, International Monetary Fund

SAMUEL SCHWEIZER *(Switzerland)* Chairman, Swiss Bank Corporation

ALLAN SPROUL *(United States)* former President, Federal Reserve Bank of New York

WILHELM TEUFENSTEIN *(Austria)* Director, Oesterreichischen Investitionskredit A.G.

GRAHAM TOWERS *(Canada)* former Governor, Bank of Canada

JOSEPH H. WILLITS *(United States)* Professor, University of Pennsylvania

Board of Directors

W. RANDOLPH BURGESS, Chairman, Washington

EUGENE R. BLACK, New York City

MARCUS WALLENBERG, Stockholm

GABRIEL FERRAS, Basle

PIERRE-PAUL SCHWEITZER, Washington

Officers of the Foundation

W. RANDOLPH BURGESS, President

ALBERT S. GERSTEIN, Vice-President and Legal Counsel

GORDON WILLIAMS, Secretary

CHARLES E. JONES, Treasurer

Appendix 3
Publications

Proceedings

1964   *Economic Growth and Monetary Stability*
Lectures by Maurice Frère and Rodrigo Goméz (Available only in Spanish; English and French stocks exhausted)

1965   *The Balance Between Monetary Policy and Other Instruments of Economic Policy in a Modern Society*
Lectures by C. D. Deshmukh and Robert V. Roosa
(Available only in French and Spanish; English stocks exhausted)

1966   *The Role of the Central Banker Today*
Lecture by Louis Rasminsky
Commentaries by Donato Menichella, Stefano Siglienti, Marcus Wallenberg and Franz Aschinger
(Available only in English and Spanish; French stocks exhausted)

1967   *Economic Development—The Banking Aspects*
Lecture by David Rockefeller
Commentaries by Felipe Herrera and Shigeo Horie
(Available in English, French and Spanish)

1968   *Central Banking and Economic Integration*
Lecture by M. W. Holtrop
Commentary by Lord Cromer
(Available only in English and Spanish; French stocks exhausted)

Other Publications

The Per Jacobsson Literary Inheritance
reprint of article by Erin E. Jucker-Fleetwood which appeared in Vol. XIX—1966—Fasc. 4 KYKLOS—The International Review for Social Sciences—Basle
(Available from the Foundation in English only and in limited quantities)